FIND YOUR HEART,
FOLLOW YOUR HEART

Get to the Heart of What Matters and Create
Your Abundant, Authentic, Joyful Life

Keri J. Olson

BALBOA.
PRESS

A DIVISION OF HAY HOUSE

Balboa Press books may be ordered through booksellers or by contacting:

Balboa Press
A Division of Hay House
1663 Liberty Drive
Bloomington, IN 47403
www.balboapress.com
1 (877) 407-4847

Because of the dynamic nature of the Internet, any web addresses or links contained in this book may have changed since publication and may no longer be valid. The views expressed in this work are solely those of the author and do not necessarily reflect the views of the publisher, and the publisher hereby disclaims any responsibility for them.

The author of this book does not dispense medical advice or prescribe the use of any technique as a form of treatment for physical, emotional, or medical problems without the advice of a physician, either directly or indirectly. The intent of the author is only to offer information of a general nature to help you in your quest for emotional and spiritual well-being. In the event you use any of the information in this book for yourself, which is your constitutional right, the author and the publisher assume no responsibility for your actions.

Print information available on the last page.

ISBN: 978-1-5043-8447-6 (sc)
ISBN: 978-1-5043-8449-0 (hc)
ISBN: 978-1-5043-8448-3 (e)

Library of Congress Control Number: 2017911226

Balboa Press rev. date: 07/17/2017

For Larry, with all of my heart.

CONTENTS

BE STILL YOUR HEART

FOLLOW YOUR HEART

FOREWORD

Keri Olson is a woman of deep spirit and blazing courage, heart, and soul buffeted by difficulty, uncertainty, illness, and loss—but never defeated. Divorce, three cancer diagnoses, as well as brain and spinal tumors that caused temporary paralysis: she's been through the gauntlet—but never defeated.

Instead of succumbing to resentment, fear, and anger, Keri opened her heart, delving deep, challenging herself to transform suffering into wholeness, wisdom, and health. This was the first step on her journey to *Find Your Heart, Follow Your Heart* and inspiration for this book.

You'd never know the depths of her suffering from her beautiful smile and gentle manner.

I first spoke with Keri as part of a Clarity Coaching session. Keri's thinking was expanding. Intuitively, she felt on the cusp of "something amazing." Prior to our conversation, she kept finding hearts (or they found her) everywhere. I encouraged her to follow those hearts—signs from the universe to follow her own heart.

Keri sought my coaching help to accomplish three goals: To be ready and able to respond positively when that "something amazing" occurred, to understand the role of hearts in her life, and to figure out how she could create a new career of writing and speaking about joy, gratitude, and abundance. (Lord knows, the world could use a lot more of that wonderful trilogy.)

We worked together to find a path to her "something amazing"— and found it. During our coaching session, Keri had that "aha" moment.

The roadmap was already inside of her. It's inside all of us. All she needed to do was follow her heart.

That journey is detailed in this book.

Through the marvelous essays, insightful observations, anecdotes, and affirmations in *Find Your Heart, Follow Your Heart*, you will find your roadmap to the heart of what matters so you, too, can create an authentic, heartfelt, spiritual life filled with abundance, joy, love, and meaning. And who doesn't want that?

Read *Find Your Heart, Follow Your Heart*. Savor Keri's wisdom, experiences, advice, and insights. When she challenges you to answer big questions about life and yourself, do it. Yes, it may be hard at times, but the rewards are great—and they last a lifetime.

Dr. Ellen Albertson, PhD, The Grow and Glow Coach

ACKNOWLEDGMENTS

Writing is a solitary experience, but it is greatly benefited by the influence of others.

I would like to express my heartfelt thanks to those who supported my writing of this book: my loving husband, Larry McCoy, who is always there to cheer me on; Pam Hillmer Marquie, who shared with me her vivid dream about this book; and Mary Pat Elsen and Robin Whyte for their expert review and helpful critique of my manuscript.

I am also grateful to: my late parents, Chuck and Barb Naidl, who showed me what it means to live an abundant, authentic, joyful life; my teachers and professors who cultivated and encouraged my love of writing; and to my family and friends who make my world a better place every day.

INTRODUCTION TO
A HEARTFELT JOURNEY

Y ou are on an amazing, exciting journey that is uniquely yours.
Your journey offers a multitude of interesting paths along the way, each with the potential for its own adventure and reward. The paths you choose can lead you closer to finding and following your heart and discovering the joy and abundance that come from being your authentic self.

At times, however, it may feel as if you're marching in place more than moving forward. The next step is needed, but it's unclear.

What to do? Ask questions.

By asking questions, contemplating them, and then thoughtfully and honestly writing down your answers, you can gain clarity to help you find your way. Your answers can illuminate your path and help you develop a successful road map to an abundant, authentic, joyful life.

The word "heart" is used frequently in phrases to explain our emotions and to describe those who are special to us, everything from broken heart to grateful heart to dear heart to sweetheart.

Find Your Heart, Follow Your Heart is a series of essays and affirmations around heart-inspired themes and phrases, with each essay followed by a set of associated questions. The essays tell of my experiences and my thoughts about each heart-themed topic. My essays are intended to fuel your thinking about how each of the topics might relate to your life.

The affirmations are positive declarations to help you articulate what you want. What you think has a profound effect on what physically manifests in your life. Each affirmation is stated in the present tense to help you send a powerful and positive message to the universe. When those affirmations are stated in the present tense with confidence, conviction, and gratitude, it is as if they have already come true. What you affirm you attract.

The questions following each essay invite your contemplation and examination in order to better understand your deeper self, hear what's calling you, help you set priorities, and create the life you want. Your responses to those questions will enhance your understanding of what's important to you and help propel you forward on your personal journey.

I've used those same questions for my own life's examination, and I revisit them periodically to make sure I'm on the right track. I am the survivor of three cancer diagnoses, as well as a benign brain tumor and a benign spinal tumor that caused temporary paralysis. While my experiences with illness haven't defined me, they have caused me to go deep within my heart. It's there where I've found and continue to find the answers that create and shape my abundant, authentic, joyful life.

Throughout this book, you'll see photographs I've taken of hearts, including stones and other heart-shaped items that seem to land in my path on my daily walks, as if they're waiting to find me. I hope the photographs give you inspiration.

What this book intends to offer you is a process, so take your time. Sit in the quiet. Read the affirmations and essays. Consider the questions. Contemplate your responses and then write them down in a journal or notebook. That way, you'll have the space to continue your writing exploration. (Refer to "Moving Forward with Your Whole Heart" at the end of this book.)

The important thing is to give yourself the time you need to consider, write, and study your responses. What do your words tell you?

So that's what this book is all about: a collection of heartfelt essays, affirmations, and photos, along with questions to stimulate your heartfelt responses to probing and pertinent questions.

As you turn each page, I hope you gain clarity and get to the heart of what matters to you. Ultimately, I hope you find your heart, follow your heart, and enjoy the journey as you create your very own abundant, authentic, joyful life.

FIND YOUR HEART

I'm finding my way. I identify what's important to me. I know with confidence what I consider to be achievement and success. My hopes and dreams that have been protected deep inside of me are now manifesting themselves in exciting and new ways. I assess as I go on this amazing journey, setting priorities and looking ahead. My goal is to find my authentic self. I embrace who I am with enthusiasm and love. I'm finding my heart.

1. FIND YOUR HEART

> I'm a seeker. When I'm still and silent, I receive clarity
> for my search. I also allow what is seeking me to
> find me.

Life is like a game of hide-and-seek. Some of what we search for is hidden in plain sight, and some can be found in unexpected places. As the years go by, I go deeper to seek the answers, for they're often already hidden inside of me. The older I get, the more my search gives way to what was actually seeking me all the while. I imagine there is universality to my experience.

There are those natural transitions in life when we spend more time in contemplation, search, and discovery: graduation, marriage, job changes, the birth of a child, a cross-country move, illness, retirement, or the death of a loved one.

Sometimes I'm not so much the active seeker as the one who's being sought. When I'm still and silent, I receive the illumination of clarity for my search and hear the active voice of what might be seeking me. It might be a new direction, a new insight to consider, or a new action to take that will forever chart a changed course for my life.

One Sunday, my pastor spoke about following your call. She suggested we need to listen to the call and heed it, even when it doesn't follow what we had intended or planned for our lives. At such times, we're being sought.

Her words made me think of the twists and turns that have come into my life and how often I thought I knew where the path was taking me—only to find it wasn't where I was supposed to be at all.

There are benefits to surrendering from our preconceived notions and plans. I seldom like to surrender fully because I value having a sense of control. When I do surrender, I allow life to do its thing. I allow myself to be sought rather than to be the seeker.

When I move intentionally and with my whole being into a new, sweet place of surrender, I let go of the sense of control I usually carry on my shoulders. Consequently, the weight of my burdens lessens and often completely disappears.

As a result of that intentional action on my part, amazing things happen. When I don't force things to go a certain way (the way I think they should go), a better way makes itself known. I see life as a series of curvy paths. The straight lines no longer look quite as attractive. By allowing for some serendipity and synchronicity, a new way of seeing and being unfolds.

So it was when I started dating my husband. I was recovering from a previous year that had included a divorce, a mastectomy (my second in less than five years), and chemotherapy. I was gaunt and pale and trying to figure out how to move my life forward after loss and illness. I let myself be completely flat-chested without trying to hide the fact that I had undergone bilateral mastectomies by the age of thirty-five. I wore a wig in a hairstyle that was foreign to me in order to hide the baldness that had come with treatment. As soon as I had enough wispy fuzz growing on my head, I removed the wig. Despite the emotional and physical trauma I had experienced, I wanted to be in a loving relationship. Rather than dwell on it, however, I let go and focused instead on my healing. It was at that same time that I began serving on a committee through our local chamber of commerce. Among those seated at the table was the new executive director of the city's local theater. After attending a few committee meetings together, the theater director asked me out, much to my surprise. Although I didn't look what I'd call my best, Larry saw beyond my flat chest, my budding hair, my pale skin, and my gaunt frame and decided I was worth a date. My letting go of a particular outcome led to an enduring and loving relationship with Larry, one that has lasted twenty-four years and counting.

Whatever is seeking you may not be a life partner, a career path, or a new city in which to live. It might be as simple (or perhaps as difficult) as being a source of love and light in the lives of others, bringing words of hope during ordinary and extraordinary times. You may be called to do something you could never have imagined for yourself.

How will you know if you've found your heart? Be still. Be. Listen carefully. As the answers come, see how they resonate with you. There may be some surprises. You may resist what you hear. But if you can accept and embrace the answers you receive, begin to move forward. Set goals and identify the first steps toward achieving them.

The more you stop what you're doing, quiet your mind, and listen deeply, the more you'll be able to hear the true words of your calling— the finding of your heart. Then and only then will you know the path to follow.

What am I seeking that would make my life more meaningful and purposeful right now? What is seeking me? What are my goals? What first steps might I take in order to achieve them?

2. HOPEFUL HEART

I have dreams for my life. I take positive action toward
them every day, even if they're small steps.

E veryone is talking about having a bucket list these days—a list of
those things you hope to accomplish before the end of your life,
such as learning to play the piano or traveling to Paris.

Although I consider myself to be pragmatic, there is a dreamer
inside of me just as there is in everyone. I don't have a bucket list exactly,
but I do have ideas and dreams for my life. I hope I'll always have dreams
and aspirations. Their good energy propels me into each new day with
anticipation.

Developing our dreams is an exciting and energetic process. Deep
inside each of our hearts is that special and sacred place where our
dreams and aspirations are born and nurtured. They're in a constant
process of forming and growing until they're ready to burst forth. The
process cannot and should not be ignored, for dreams will have their way
of tugging at us until we acknowledge and feed them.

What dreams do you carry in that safe, secret, and sacred place in
your heart? What dreams are waiting to burst forth? How do you plan
to manifest them? What is stopping you?

Be bold. Take action. Don't be scared by the prospect of a huge leap.
Take a small step. The first step can seem hard, but doing nothing at
all is even harder. An unrealized dream will only lead to regret. A small
step will propel you forward and build your confidence, leading to the
next step and the next until your dream is a reality.

Getting to that first small step will take some thought about your way of thinking. We all tend to get stuck in our ruts and find change a fearful prospect. By embracing change, however, which is always with you anyway, you release some of the tension. And if you accept that your attempts might lead to some mistakes and even failures along the way, you'll become less fearful. You might even end up on a path you would have never seen for yourself. What's there to lose for trying? It's all about learning and having fun, being curious, and creating the conditions in your life to have and realize your dreams, regardless of your age or circumstances.

A curious mind is a fertile mind, creating an ideal environment for dream making. A handy dose of curiosity and a desire to learn new things make the process more enjoyable and may actually help shape your dreams in ways you couldn't anticipate or expect.

My late father lived his dreams. From childhood on, he had a curiosity and respect for reptiles, especially snakes. Dad grew up during the Great Depression, and his mother was widowed young. With the untimely death of my grandfather, Grandma found herself solely responsible for the well-being of her four young children, with my father being the only son. As a boy, Dad discovered a fascination for reptiles. By the time he was in his teens, and then a young man, his interest had grown even deeper. He studied reptiles, made drawings of their anatomy, wrote notes in journals, read scholarly books, and even kept cages of local snakes in their home. Despite not being particularly fond of his pets, my grandmother encouraged Dad's passion and even helped feed and care for the snakes, moving their cages carefully from window to window to ensure they got the right amount of warmth and light.

Dad's interest in reptiles didn't wane during his stint in the US Army. He managed to find time to hunt and learn more about reptiles from faraway places, including the Mojave Desert and Germany where he was stationed during World War II. Following the war, Dad dedicated his time to increasing his knowledge and fostering relationships with a network of experts on the subject of reptiles.

Shortly after my parents married, they bought rural property in Wisconsin where they built their own reptile farm as a place for education about these oft-misunderstood creatures. At the same time, Dad also embarked on a successful decades-long career of lecturing in schools and other venues across the continental United States about the virtues and value of reptiles in the ecosystem. Everywhere he went, Dad was known as "the snake man." His popular presentations and programs were given praise and high marks. He became a frequent recipient of favorable print and broadcast publicity coverage as a reptile expert and educator. My mother and I had many opportunities to travel with him on his school program circuits, which provided a rich education for me even before I was old enough to attend school myself.

Throughout his life, my dad kept learning through reading, study, and discussions with professors, naturalists, herpetologists, conservationists, zoo administrators, college graduate students, and reptile enthusiasts. They were all frequent visitors to our reptile farm. I don't believe that Dad left this earth with a bucket list. Step by step throughout his life, he pursued his dreams and saw his aspirations turn into reality.

The ability to dream and aspire is evergreen. It doesn't matter at what point you are in life. The desire to experience life as an adventurer invites you to learn something new each day. Think about what appeals to your curiosity and interests. Listen to your dreams. Believe in your aspirations. Make them happen, step by step. It is out of your dreams that wonderful, new things will be born.

What aspirations, hopes, and dreams do I have for my life? What first steps might I take in order to achieve them?

3. HEART OF SUCCESS

I'm successful, regardless of how much money or how
many material possessions I have.

The theme of our church's annual stewardship drive one year was
about discovering joy through simplicity and generosity. The
moment I learned of that theme, I knew it was meant for me because I
love a life of generosity and simplicity. I believe there is great joy in the
act of giving, especially when coupled with an attitude of gratitude for
the blessing of abundance.

To kick off the stewardship drive, my pastor spoke of our society's
definition of success as a life of consuming, acquiring, and buying.
In her words, the American dream has become something of an
American nightmare. She talked about affluenza, that state of extreme
consumerism that leads to debt and overwork in an attempt to get out
of the debt. She talked about "credit-itis," when materialism leads to
buying more on credit than one can afford. She talked about our desire
for more that is never satisfied.

Although I grew up in an instant-gratification era, my parents were
products of the Great Depression. They understood what it meant
to do without, and they instilled in me their value of frugality. They
lived below their means and did so happily. They lived without fear
of suffering from lack. Consequently, I have very few needs and even
fewer wants. Fortunately, my husband and I have the same values, so we
happily live a frugal lifestyle together.

Each time I contemplate buying something, I stop myself before making the purchase to determine at what cost I'm willing to add one more item to my heap of possessions. Is the item a necessity or is it a whim? Will the item bring me joy or will it just be one more thing to dust, store, insure? Will it enhance my well-being? If the proposed purchase meets my criteria for justification, I buy it willingly. Then, as I bring that item into our home, I remove at least one other thing. That practice prevents me from having too much stuff and hopefully moves me closer to a simpler, more streamlined life with fewer things to own me. It's my own effort to keep away the affluenza and "credit-itis" to which my pastor spoke and to embrace the minimalism that seems natural to me.

While housecleaning one Saturday morning, I thought about how our belongings own us, how if I had less living space and fewer things, my life would be lighter. With that church stewardship season theme of discovering joy through simplicity and generosity as my inspiration, I began to concentrate even more on acquiring less for myself and giving more to others. With each step I took, I found my efforts increased my happiness.

A person needs very little to be happy. Once your basic needs are met, everything else is frosting on the cake. Happiness is not based on what you own, what you wear, what kind of car you drive, in what neighborhood you live, or what you do for a living. Happiness is attainable simply by looking at your life through a lens of gratitude, taking care of yourself, finding meaning in your work to make the world a better place, and fostering deep, lasting relationships with family and friends.

A simple, happy life is a successful life. In our society, sadly, we can be swayed by persuasive pressures to consume and overwork, creating a vicious cycle of constantly naming our wants, buying to hopefully fulfill them, and then working long hours or more than one job in order to pay for those wants.

What we have come to define as success may actually end up weighing us down with all of its baggage. When we adjust our thinking so that we can see success from different angles, we're able to discard some of that baggage, revealing a level of joy we may not have experienced for a long time. This can be particularly true if our focus has been on doing whatever is needed, including working unrealistically long hours, in order to climb the corporate ladder. We've allowed ourselves to be put on a short leash, preventing us from being fully away from our work because technology has tethered us to the desk even in our off-hours or while on vacation. Perhaps there hasn't even been time for a vacation because success meant working all of the time.

I've been guilty of not using the vacation time I earned, and I'm not proud of it. Once I realized such a lifestyle was unhealthy for me, I took steps to change my ways. My husband joined me by embracing many of those changes.

I started by scheduling long weekends off from work, using my vacation days as opportunities for mini-getaways, staycations, and retreats. I began muting my smartphone the minute I got home from work, checking it only at intervals in the evening and on weekends. I stopped looking at my smartphone altogether at least one hour before bedtime. I began to incorporate time each day for meditation, reading, play, and exercise.

My husband and I switched to a healthy, plant-based diet of whole foods, and we decided to reserve eating out only for special occasions. Consequently, we found a renewed joy in preparing our healthy meals together at home.

We stopped attending the high volume of events we had historically attended in our community. That one effort afforded us significantly increased unstructured time together. Now, when my husband and I do attend an event, it's a special experience—not just part of the weekly grind. Although no longer attending all of their activities, we continue to support those same charitable organizations with our monetary gifts and volunteer time.

With each healthy decision we've made, regardless of what society would suggest as a so-called successful lifestyle, our happiness has increased.

Eventually, Larry and I changed careers after evaluating how much income we needed for our living expenses. We determined it was more important to have time to do the things that had meaning to us as individuals and as a couple. Now, our lives are more intentional. Instead of bumping haphazardly into each other after hours of work, meetings, and events, we now have time to take long walks, pursue hobbies together, and discuss subjects of mutual interest in depth. We read aloud to each other. We have more time to volunteer. We get together with our friends more often.

For me, abundance is achieved through purpose, passion, and living a meaningful life, regardless of the size of my paycheck or the number of rungs climbed on the corporate ladder. It means being vigilant about my definition of success so I always remember that I don't need much to be happy.

A happy, grateful life is a successful life. It's a discovery of joy through simplicity, love, and generosity. If you remember that, you'll always feel successful.

How do I define success? What does it mean to have an abundant life? What roles do money and possessions have in my life?

4. SECRET HEART

I'm true to myself. My inner and outer selves are congruent.

While driving in the lush countryside, I noticed a barn with an intriguing sign affixed to its roof. The sign featured just one word: harmony. I don't know the reason for the sign, but I was taken by the message all the same. As I drove along, it gave me something to ponder. Just how much do I seek harmony in my life, a simple balance of work and play, seriousness and silliness, activity and rest, my inner being and the outer being I show the world? Do I accept me for who I am? Am I true to who I am at all times?

As a young teenage girl, there were those occasions when I wanted to be part of the "in" crowd, that group of girls who seemed to have everything. They were beautiful, popular, smart, slender, well dressed, and athletic—or so I thought. If I had gotten into their heads and hearts, however, I likely would have found some of the same insecurities I felt during those years. As I look back on it now, it all seems rather silly, but it was an important part of that awkward time in my life between childhood and adulthood when I was growing, changing, exploring, and becoming who I was and questioning if I liked what I found. Between my junior and senior years in high school, it struck me finally that I didn't need to be like others in order to be liked. I needed to be myself fully and celebrate my uniqueness. Only then would my inner and outer selves be in harmony and would my true colors show and shine.

Speaking of colors, there was an exercise going around for a while on the Internet, inviting you to respond to a series of questions in order to discover your true color aura. Although I normally take a pass on such quizzes, I decided on a whim to complete the questionnaire. In a few minutes, a message popped up that my aura was blue. While some of the characteristics of blue-aura folks were a bit of a stretch for me, the skeptic in me was somewhat surprised to see many aspects of myself in what I read. People with a predominantly blue aura need to be liked and accepted. In their deep need for peace and harmony, they seek to create conflict-free surroundings. They are the caretakers of others, taking that responsibility and all others seriously, which can lead to a tendency toward caution and worry. Blue-aura people are tidy by nature and can even become overwhelmed by untidiness. They are honest, trustworthy, and sincere.

What does it all mean? Probably nothing. The important thing is that we honor who we are as unique, discrete individuals. Trying to be part of the popular crowd or keep up with our neighbors only causes disharmony. Your authentic self is your true color, no matter what an Internet quiz tries to tell you.

Take a pulse check every now and again and examine whether your inner and outer selves are in alignment. Make adjustments as necessary, so your authenticity can speak. It may be some of the nicest harmony you'll ever hear.

Am I the same person inside as I portray on the outside? What might I do today to bring my outer and inner selves into alignment? What would it take to be my authentic self?

5. PUT YOUR HEART INTO IT

I know what's important to me. I dedicate my attention
to it.

L ife is filled with somedays, gonna-dos, and hope-to-bes. There's
always tomorrow to make time for those things, right? If you're
waiting for that perfect job or that perfect home or that perfect amount
of money or that perfect life partner, reconsider your thinking. What
are your priorities? What's most important to you?

In the 1970s, there was a popular sitcom called *One Day at a Time*.
While I watched the show regularly as a teenager, I never really thought
about the implications of the show's title. Indeed, we're all given but
one day at a time. How we use each of those single days is the stuff of
contemplation and careful action, especially as we grow older and we
realize those days have been numbered all along.

Recently when I was given sad news about a friend's health and then
learned of another friend's death, I was reminded of the importance of
having my priorities straight and living with a heart full of gratitude. I was
reminded of the importance of living life with intention and compassion,
of pursuing my gonna-dos and wanna-bes while opportunity remains. I
was reminded to enjoy each moment, soak up each aspect of it, paying
attention to every detail.

I see that wisdom played out over and over again during visits with
friends who are older than I—people who have lived long, full lives and
who are at a quieter, more introspective stage now. They enjoy each
moment as they see the number of years ahead of them wane. One such

friend commented one day about sitting at her kitchen window, losing track of time as she watches nature's changes unfold. She spoke with reverence of the deer and fox, the blooming of early spring wildflowers, and the ebb and flow of the seasons. She told me she likes to listen to the wind. At the time, we were deep in conversation about the magnificent eruption of spring, from the fragrances of the season to the song of the birds to the beauty of the wildflowers blooming in the woods next to her home. As one well attuned to nature's subtleties, my friend knows to listen to the wind, to be present to it and its messages.

It all comes down to our putting our hearts in a place of attention and intention and focusing on right now. None of us know what tomorrow will bring or even the next minute for that matter. There are no guarantees we will get to that perfect time in our lives when the stars align and we can then, finally, pursue what we dreamed of doing or become the person we wished to be.

Instead, look to today—this moment, now.

We have the ability to live our lives one day at a time with the fullness of our attention that it deserves. I'm trying not to multitask or worry or regret these days. Instead, I'm trying to live as I did when I was a child before the myriad adult distractions were placed in my head as my so-called grown-up priorities. I'm trying to identify and pursue those gonna-dos and hope-to-bes while I have the drive and desire to do so. I'm trying to adopt the wisdom of my elder friends who have slowed down so they can see beauty in nature's changes and listen to the wind. Admittedly, it all takes effort, but the gift of living one day at a time with joy, appreciation, and gusto is well worth it.

Make time to consider your priorities. Consider how you will use this one precious day to do the things and be with the people most important to you.

What are the five most important priorities in my life? What action could I take each day to care for and feed those priorities? How might I simplify my life to focus on the people, things, and activities that are most important to me?

6. BRAVE HEART

I do the brave, right thing—even when it seems hard.
My life is in harmony with my values.

I once met a cat named Courage. His human companion told me the
cat was normally fearful when strangers came around and would
immediately run and hide.

For some reason that day, Courage and I hit it off. He stayed put
in his little kitty bed and allowed me to pet him and scratch him under
his chin. He never once ran away to hide. Instead, he seemed content
and curious at the same time, comfortable enough with me to stay put,
stretch out, and take me in.

Courage the cat got me to thinking about the depth of my own
courage. When confronted with something new, do I usually run
and hide? Or do I see the situation for what it is and allow myself to
become comfortable with it, stretching out and taking it in just as my
cat-friend did?

One Sunday, our worship service was dedicated to the subject
of bravery. We responsively read words of dawning understandings,
stretching spirits, and reaching toward God's bright and beckoning
wisdom. The biblical passages admonished the reader to be strong,
courageous, brave, and steadfast and to be on guard.

After the service, several of my fellow parishioners and I talked
about the things we were encountering in our lives that caused us to
reach into our very depths for some bravery. It made me think of the
Cowardly Lion in *The Wizard of Oz* who was seeking courage. Don't

we all recognize a bit of the Cowardly Lion in ourselves as we navigate the challenges of life, searching all around and inside us for that bit of bravery that will answer our dilemmas, comfort our spirits, renew our strength, and deter our fears?

That is where conviction comes in. Have faith in yourself and in your beliefs and values. Whatever you need to take on, even when afraid, you can if you stay grounded in what's important to you. Have the courage to say what you believe, even when your voice feels small and shaky and you're not sure how others will feel about you and your words once you utter them. Speak from a place of truth. Speak from a place of love. If you follow your moral compass, you will sleep well, knowing that your words and decisions were honest, true, and respectful.

Each of us has the power to look fear in the eye and display our own courage. Take a lesson from Courage the cat and trust your instincts as to whether something or someone feels right or not. See newness and change as the opportunities they are. Rely on your values to help you make the right decision or to take on that difficult moment. You can do it. Have courage.

In what area of my life do I need to be brave? What constructive action might I take to address the situation with courage and conviction?

ratification, *n.* satisfaction; entertainment; fulfillment; diversion, ease, comfort; indulgence, consumption. See PLEASURE. *Ant.,* see

rating, *n.* lattice, openwork, grillwork, grid.

GRATITUDE

Nouns—gratitude, gratefulness, thankfulness; indebtedness; acknowledgment, recognition, thanksgiving; thanks, praise, benediction; *Te Deum,* WORSHIP, grace; thank-offering; requital.

Verbs—be grateful, thank; give, render, return, offer *or* tender acknowledge, requite; thank *or* bless one's stars.

Adjectives—grateful, thankful, appreciative, obliged, beholden, indebted, under obligation.

Interjections—thanks! much obliged! thank you! thank Heaven! Heaven be praised! thanks a million! *gracias*! *merci*!

Antonym, see INGRATITUDE.

grave, *n. & adj.* —*n.* burial place, sepulcher, tomb, mausoleum. S —*adj.* important, weighty

BLESS YOUR HEART

My heart is filled with gratitude and appreciation for all I have and all I'm given. As my appreciation grows, so does my abundance. I love myself for who I am, who I've been, and who I will be. As a measure of self-love and self-respect, I ensure my relationships are healthy, trusting, and nurturing. I radiate love within and without. The more love I give, the more love I feel in return. My world is filled with generosity, goodness, and kindness. My heart is blessed beyond measure.

7. GRATEFUL HEART

I'm grateful. My blessings are always greater than my
worries.

It's easy to be grateful when things are going well. It's a lot harder to
count your blessings when the way is rough.

On the last evening of my mom's life, I was alone with her, seated
by her bed, witnessing her moving more and more into that mysterious
transition we call death. I was caught up in a mix of memories, sadness,
loneliness, and trepidation, for I had never been with anyone when they
passed away, especially someone I loved so much.

While lost in a swirl of mixed emotions, a dear friend walked into
Mom's hushed and darkened room. Instead of delivering the platitudes
I'd become used to hearing (and, sadly, accustomed to saying myself
when there seemed nothing else to say at such difficult times), my friend
surprised me by taking my hand, placing something into it, and then,
with her fingers clasped tightly around mine, she said simply and gently,
"Give thanks." When she released her hand and I opened mine, I found
that my friend had slipped into my palm a small brass leaf embossed
with the words, "Give Thanks."

My friend went on to explain that during my justifiable grief, I had
the opportunity to give thanks for having had such a wonderful mother
and such an unusually close relationship with her. She also reminded
me I had the blessing of having walked Mom's final journey with her to
where we found ourselves now.

The notion of giving thanks hadn't crossed my mind as I tortured myself between fond memories and the sad finality of goodbye. But my friend's words and her gift touched my heart and changed my perspective. I did indeed have so much for which to be grateful. That new state of understanding in which I found myself, thanks to my friend's wisdom, led me to accept what was and to work with it, not against it. Consequently, Mom's dying became a new beginning for her and for me.

Following my mother's passing, I began a ritual of listing three blessings in my life upon waking and three more blessings before falling asleep at night.

The act of bookending my day with gratitude, thinking of the good that awaits me and the good that took place during my waking hours, has proven to be a valuable exercise. When I begin and end my day in a state of gratitude, it frames my way of thinking for all of my other waking hours. My outlook on life becomes more optimistic. Even my sleep is more restful.

There are many ways to express gratitude. Here are three suggestions: 1. Write in a daily gratitude journal. 2. Use a prompt to remind yourself to be grateful, such as whenever you're at a stoplight, every time the phone rings, or each time you open the refrigerator door. 3. Keep a gratitude jar by writing on small pieces of paper something for which you're thankful every day or every few days. Then review the contents at the end of the year and reflect on your many blessings. Find a method that's right for you.

If we spend our days steeped in gratitude, they'll be so filled with joy there'll be little time for complaint or worry. When we recognize all we have, the need for more seems pretty pointless.

Every new day provides opportunities to rejoice and give thanks. My late mom used to remind me of a biblical passage anytime I seemed ungrateful: "This is the day which the Lord hath made; we will rejoice and be glad in it" (Psalm 118:24 KJV).

Gratitude is the open door to abundance. It changes everything. There is always, always something to be thankful for.

What am I grateful for? What three blessings can I name in my life right now? What gratitude practice might I begin today to focus on my blessings?

8. GENEROUS HEART

> I'm thankful when others are generous with me. I'm
> also thankful when I have the opportunity to give.

I learned a lesson in generosity when I was in elementary school that has stayed with me throughout the decades. When I was in the fourth and fifth grades, the principal would ask me to escort younger children from our school to a nearby store with instructions to fit them with winter boots, coats, hats, mittens, and the like. Time and time again, she would place money in my hand and send me with a young charge to that store, which carried everything from clothing to furniture. The principal was likely using her own hard-earned money to clothe those schoolchildren appropriately for the elements. Her generous heart touched mine profoundly at a young age.

For the past few years, Girl Scouts in our community have organized annual drives that resulted in the collection of new and gently used coats, snow pants, hats, scarves, mittens, and winter boots for local children in need. Their thoughtful efforts have reminded me of the gestures of my elementary school principal so long ago. I'm grateful for this new generation of generous hearts. There was need then, and there is need now. That need can be filled when we spread the light of love and generosity to one another.

Often, it is children who show us how to be generous and kind. While on the last lap of my walk one evening, I passed by a house where two women were seated on the front step. They were accompanied by a little girl of no more than four years of age. I smiled and spoke to the trio. The two ladies replied with a friendly greeting, smiling back at me. Then one of the women encouraged the little girl to say hello. Instead of greeting me, the little girl ran toward me, hand outstretched in a tight fist. As she approached me, she opened her hand, revealing four little red stones and two blue. She told me in her sweet, little-girl voice that she wanted me to have them. She carefully poured her precious cargo into my grown-up hand and then ran back to the two ladies. I thanked her for sharing her precious gift with me and assured her I would cherish them. How lovely it is when someone gives so selflessly and joyfully, even to a complete stranger. My life was touched by that child's wisdom, and I was indeed the richer.

Such displays of generosity remind me of the song "This Little Light of Mine." One recent Sunday, it was delivered with perfection by the children's choir at my church. The children's earnest expressions and sweet voices encouraged all present to let their lights shine. Through their unfiltered enthusiasm, those tiny ones delivered the big message that we are each given gifts, riches, and talents that are uniquely our own. It is a blessing and indeed a privilege to contribute those riches, talents, and gifts for the greater good, regardless of how small or insignificant we may believe them to be. The light you may think is but a tiny flicker might be a beacon for someone else.

We all have something precious to give for the betterment of our neighborhood, community, and world. I challenge you to find those organizations and causes whose values resonate with your own and then give of yourself. You will be better for it, and the world will be better too.

What might you give? It could be a tangible item, such as a winter coat, hat, or scarf. It could be a cash donation. It could be your time. Your generosity, given in any form, has the profound capacity to cast light into the shadows.

I will never forget my elementary school principal, the Girl Scouts, or the little girl who gave me her precious red and blue stones. They taught me important lessons about how we all have the capacity to reach out compassionately and generously in significant and light-filled ways.

What do I have to offer to another person, to an organization, or to my community? What can I give through my time, talent, or treasure, such as donations of cash or goods, and to whom?

9. KIND HEART

I use my energies well by focusing my thoughts, words,
and deeds on kindness.

It's been said that one of the most powerful ways to counter the trials
and cruelties of life is to be kind. Kindness is indeed an antidote to
so much of what ails us.

As time goes by, I see being kind as more and more important. If
I'm not kind, then what am I? What better way to live life than to be
kind or to see kindness in others? What better way to disarm and defeat
catastrophes and injustices than to find every opportunity to be kind?
As the yard sign says on one of my walking routes, kindness matters.

I had the opportunity to deliver a message to some graduating high
school seniors, a portion of which was dedicated to the importance of
kindness. I told those young people who were ready to take on the world that
as they moved along life's journey, they should always remember to be kind.

There will be rewards of many types that will come to them—new
jobs, career advancements, bonuses, and the like. However, I told them
that by taking the time to be kind to everyone (even when it's downright
hard), they will receive some of the greatest satisfaction and happiness.

I also reminded them to be grateful along the way. It's natural to
get caught up in worries, concerns, and what-ifs, but they hold little
power over your path or destiny when you stop to be grateful for what
you already have. Gratitude feeds kindness. Kindness feeds gratitude.

Throughout the years, life has taught me that the lessons will never
end. We all carry dreams in our hearts, regardless of our age or stage in

life. Our passions tell us who we really are. We should pay attention to what gives us joy and honor those things with the investment of our time and dedication. Adopting an attitude of gratitude makes every day a gift to be cherished. We create our own happiness. Being remembered for our kindness means more than any accolade, award, or degree.

Fortunately, we have many opportunities to see kindness in this world and to learn from them. Watching the evening news on any given night, however, might make you think otherwise because only the most violent, horrific, extraordinary, and troubling events seem to be worth a sound bite. We must direct our focus to what is kind and good. Looking for it will surely help us find it.

I witness kind hearts, words, and deeds every day in my ordinary life: a neighbor reaching out to another neighbor, adults tutoring children, businesses organizing food pantry drives, and teenagers volunteering at a nursing home.

I think of my own late mother when I think of models of kindness. Perhaps it was the nurse in her that remained long after her retirement. Perhaps it was in her DNA. Whatever it was, Mom was kindness personified in thought, word, and deed. As Mom's health failed and her body steadily weakened from cancer, she could still be seen pushing nursing home residents' wheelchairs, consoling someone who was sad, and sitting quietly with a friend whose own health was failing. At the visitation before her memorial service, person after person described Mom as gentle, an excellent teacher, a respected nurse, someone who was always kind. In the end, it won't be the rewards or other earthly treasures that will matter. Our legacy will be determined by who we were as people: how generous, compassionate, loving, and kind we were, especially to those who will never be in a position to repay us for what we've done for them.

The world truly is a kind place. Sometimes we just have to look a little harder to find it. Surely bad things happen, but doesn't it nourish our spirits much more when we focus on the good and kind, instead of the dreary and alarming?

We all have opportunities to learn from the examples of other kind souls. They inspire us to lighten another's load and contribute in our own way to the greater good. There is always room for a kind heart, a kind word, and a kind deed. Kindness is the answer. Kindness matters.

What kindness did I experience yesterday? What one thing can I do today to extend kindness to someone else?

10. GENTLE HEART

I'm happy with who I am. I release self-critical thoughts, set healthy limits, and celebrate my uniqueness. I wholeheartedly engage in self-love.

"**H**ow are you?"

"I'm so busy," said dramatically with a drawn-out sigh.

"I understand. I'm so busy too," said with a furrowed brow and a knowing nod, followed by an even longer sigh.

Does that conversation sound familiar? Being busy seems to be in fashion these days—the busier, the better. It's a strange badge of honor when we brag about dragging ourselves around sleep deprived, never able to catch up with proper rest or relaxation. Being busy somehow makes us seem important. Being busy with what we are busying ourselves with makes us seem even more important.

There was a period of three months when I was particularly— you guessed it—busy. I was overcommitted with three simultaneous professional endeavors, and I was overdoing just to keep up. I knew it, but I had made a promise, and the dutiful part of me wanted to see my responsibilities through. By the time I was finished with my obligations, every part of my being felt finished too. I was overtired in mind, body, and spirit. It took me the better part of the next three months to rebuild my strength and find my groove again.

In retrospect, I see that by permitting myself to enter into such a state of busyness, I wasn't exercising my best judgment, and my life was severely out of balance.

When my life is in balance, things move smoothly and easily, and I move smoothly and easily right along with them. I'm energized and enthusiastic while I'm immersed in my activities. I'm happy with who I am and where I am in my life. I say yes only to those things that seem right to me, not because I feel obligated. Therefore, I'm busy enough to feel productive and purposeful but not overcommitted. I'm able to complete the task at hand without stress and have time to spare for thinking, dreaming, and pondering.

It's so easy, too easy to say yes to things when the better response may be to say no. We've been trained to say yes. Somehow, by saying no, we fear we'll let ourselves and others down or we'll miss out on something, that whole FOMO (fear of missing out) thing. What's the big deal about missing out on something anyway?

By saying no to something, you automatically make room for something else more important or more enjoyable. By setting limits, you grant yourself permission to better utilize your energy and time. It's better to be honest and simply say no when that is what your heart is telling you. When you're invited to add something to your life, ask yourself if saying yes will help or hamper. Does the decision make your gut expand or contract? If your gut contracts and tells you no, heed its message.

Remember that saying no doesn't define you negatively. It has nothing to do with your talents or your accomplishments or your worth. Saying no is simply a self-respectful decision. It opens up opportunities to saying yes to what is better for you. In turn, your time will be more wisely spent.

The bottom line: Always take care of you first. That means setting limits, devoting time each day to self-care, and hearing the voice of self-compassion. It means saying no in order to leave room for all of the right yes moments in your life. Such self-care is essential. It's vital to your health and well-being.

While you're practicing saying no, learn to say no, too, to the self-critical thoughts that meander through your mind. They're just as destructive, if not more so, than overcommitting your time. Rest your mind and reframe your thoughts to those of self-compassion. Transfer that self-compassion into a routine that feeds your mind, body, and spirit.

One summer evening, I took a hike with two female friends. One of the women talked about the power of our own positive energy casting out and reflecting back to us with even more positive energy. The other shared her wisdom about listening carefully to the nuances of our bodies as an ultimate measure of self-care. These two wise, gentle, remarkable women reminded me that taking care of my mind, body, and spirit is a necessary component of a life well-lived.

It's all about self-love. Love is at the heart of our being. When we love ourselves, we welcome happiness, joy, and a sense of healing in and around us. We're better able to radiate that love outward to the people and things that matter to us most.

Engage in self-love. Shower yourself with kind words. Set healthy limits. Honor your uniqueness and your gifts. Ask yourself, "What will I do to love myself today?"

Am I happy with the person I am? Do I recognize my talents and accomplishments? Do I celebrate what makes me uniquely me? What does my self-critical voice say? Do I put others' needs first to the detriment of my own? When do I say yes when I really want to say no? How might I shower myself with more love, respect, and gentleness today?

11. LOVING HEART

I'm happiest when I make time for the people I love and care about. My life is richer because of them.

I once heard of a woman described as "the rock and the soul" of her family. What a wonderful tribute to pay to someone. Our lives are fleeting and fragile. Our relationships are the glue that puts all of those fragile pieces together to form a life that is well lived and well loved.

For me, being someone's rock means you're present in the good and not-so-good times. You're steadfast, always to be counted on. Being the soul suggests you express yourself with caring, kindness, gratitude, and inclusion so that those in your midst feel loved, valued, and appreciated.

Sit back for a moment and think about those who are your rock and soul, those important people in your life who are there for you and who cast their love and compassion on you. See their faces. Hear their voices. Now think about the amount of time each day, each week that you spend with those important people. Do you allot sufficient time to them? Is the time you allot enough to truly nurture those precious relationships with the people who are your rock and soul?

During the final months of my mother's life, I dedicated a portion of each day to her. As her cancer progressed, it became necessary for her to receive the quality attention of a skilled-care facility. As much as I wanted to care for Mom at home, it wasn't to be. Once I reconciled that I couldn't be her physical caregiver, I released the guilt and decided that my remaining time with Mom was going to be that of quality over quantity. I would soak up every moment with her. Consequently, Mom and I sat together and looked at old photo albums and scrapbooks. We reminisced. We took rides into the countryside to watch spring unfold into summer. We cheered together as our favorite pro-football team won a particularly challenging game. As the end drew closer, I fed Mom. I helped dress and undress her. I read to her. We laughed and we cried. Every moment with Mom, every act I engaged in to help her was sacred. I knew I would never have that time back with her again. I wanted no regrets.

Nothing is permanent. Therefore, it's important to spend time with those we love while we can. Just as our calendars and datebooks are filled with meetings and other obligations, there should be time set aside in our calendars for those we care about.

Instead of having our heads down looking at our digital devices, why not get out an old-fashioned board game and share an afternoon of laughter with your children or grandchildren? Spend time with your mother or sister at the neighborhood coffee shop. Schedule a date with your spouse for dinner and a movie. Help your father or brother finish a home project that's been on his to-do list forever. Schedule a round of golf or a lunch date with a friend.

Time spent in conversation and laughter with those we love and care about provides some of our richest memories. In the end, we won't remember the big, expensive things we bought or the extravagant gifts we received. In fact, they'll easily get lost in the recesses of our minds. Instead, our memories will be rich because of the priceless time we spent with those who mattered to us. That is what will count then, and it is what counts now.

Who is important in my life? Do I spend as much time as I would like with those people who are important to me? Do I nurture those connections on a regular basis? How might I express my love, friendship, and appreciation for those important people in my life today?

12. HEALING HEART

> I enjoy affirming, positive relationships with the people
> in my life. If I feel the need to heal a relationship, I
> make every effort to do so. When that's not possible, I
> focus on healing myself.

Our relationships bring vibrant color to our lives.
As a child, I remember singing a song about old and new
friends being like silver and gold. My thoughts went to that old song
recently when I sat at the comfortable kitchen table, mug of steaming
herbal tea in hand, with a wonderful friend. I can chat with her about
everything important and not so important. We enjoy quiet conversation
about the weather and gardening and about illness and loss. I have
another friend whose eternal optimism and joyful disposition bring
happiness to every encounter with her. When I'm with her, I feel
buoyant. Those women are among my silver and gold friends.

I also have friends who are all shades of true blue, representing
a spectrum from azure to navy. Time may play an important role in
determining the trueness of a friendship, for time and familiarity
certainly help establish a meaningful and lasting bond. However, some
newly acquired friends can also be true, just as they can be empathetic,
faithful, and loving. Perhaps equal in importance to the length of a
friendship is the depth of that relationship, which comes from a shared
experience, something that transforms the individual and the friendship
forever. Whether new or longtime, I am blessed to have true-blue friends.

We hear often about the importance of having strong social bonds throughout life, especially as we grow older. Those relationships help us age in a healthier, happier fashion. I realize I could give up a lot, but those loving relationships with my family and friends are among my most precious possessions.

Social media have become a source for cultivating friendships. There may be veracity to those friends, but nothing replaces real, in-person encounters that transcend the good and not-so-good times. They are the friends in whom you can confide, who will hold your hand when all you can do is cry, and who can be counted on to be trustworthy and loyal.

There are also those relationships with friends or family that are not so silver, gold, or true blue. Instead, they feel muddy brown, murky gray, and downright difficult. Those relationships may be the result of personality clashes, events that caused disharmony or distrust, hurt words that were never forgiven, or apologies that never took place.

Some people see life through a negative lens. No matter what good might happen, they somehow see the downside. Whenever you're with them, they have the capacity to drag you down too. The energy seems to be sucked out of the room whenever they enter. Their judgment, criticism, or negative vibes contract, rather than expand, the space.

It's far more enjoyable to be around positive and affirming people, those who laugh easily, love generously, and radiate optimism. Surround yourself with them and you will feel positive too.

Other relationships may feel lopsided and may, if not checked, result in your feeling used and your value underappreciated. No one likes to feel valuable only when needed. That's disrespectful—plain and simple.

There should never, ever be space for abuse of any kind. Relationships require both parties to place a certain value on the relationship as a whole and on each other as individuals. If only one party is contributing and the other is merely the recipient with very little given back, it may be time for some honest conversation that clearly and respectfully spells out your concerns and encourages resolution. Such a conversation can shed much-needed light that leads to changed behavior.

If, on the other hand, that conversation does not change behavior and you find yourself continuing to be hurt, it may be time to let go of the relationship and cleanse your life of its toxicity.

I've had to do that. I never wished the person ill, but I knew the relationship could not carry on under the existing rules. It's better to respectfully wish the person well and move on. It may not be easy to sever the ties to that individual, depending on the depth of the relationship, but your time and attention will be better served elsewhere.

In the end, our relationships should lift us up, not weigh us down. Be true to you and honor your worth. Enjoy and nurture the great relationships in your life, mend those that need healing, and walk away from those that do not serve you in ways you deserve.

Are there relationships in my life that are difficult and need mending, healing, or some other action? Do I accept responsibility for my role in those relationships? What productive and healthy steps might I take to resolve any difficulties in my relationships or walk away from those that do not serve me well?

TUNE INTO YOUR HEART

I take care of my mind, body, and spirit as a high priority in my life. My well-being is important to me. Therefore, I make healthy choices. I spend time cultivating my passions and celebrating my talents. I enjoy expressing myself in creative ways that are unique to me. I value the time I spend in laughter and play. I'm a spiritual being. I dedicate time to silence as a gift of renewal. I'm calm and at peace. I freely tune into my heart, and I like what I hear.

13. HEART HEALTHY

> I honor the body with which I've been blessed. I fuel my
> energies by eating healthy food, exercising, managing
> stress, and getting adequate sleep.

I am a three-time cancer survivor. I've had two breast cancer diagnoses and a melanoma. I've also experienced two benign tumors, one in my brain and one pressing so severely on my spinal cord that I became temporarily paralyzed and had to learn to walk again. Those are the medical highlights of my adulthood, which has been interrupted every now and again by life-threatening and life-altering illnesses.

Instead of plummeting into long-term despair over these strange and uninvited challenges to my health, I decided to take control of anything I thought might be within my grasp to facilitate my overall health and well-being.

Consequently, I adopted primarily a vegan diet and eliminated nearly all processed foods from the grocery list.

I hydrate with plenty of water.

I meditate and pray to stay connected with my higher power, God, Source, the universe.

I get at least one hour of brisk walking or other aerobic activity daily. I do push-ups and other strengthening exercises. I do balancing exercises, and I stretch my muscles.

I feed my creative spirit with a variety of hobbies and interests.

I engage with family and friends and make time to socialize with them as often as possible.

I focus on positive thoughts to mitigate stress.

I engage in lifelong learning through reading, discussion groups, workshops, classes, and lectures.

I make our bedroom an uncluttered, serene, and cool haven that invites sound sleep for eight hours each night.

I stop checking my electronic devices at least one hour before bedtime.

I practice mindfulness.

While most of the lifestyle changes noted above have come quite easily to me, mindfulness remains one of my biggest challenges. I tend to have a busy brain. With each activity in which I engage, however, I increasingly direct and redirect my focus to being mindful of the moment, the experience, and the blessing. I can easily deceive myself into thinking I get ahead when multitasking. The truth is it's hard to do anything well when trying to do multiple things at once, especially while doing them quickly.

We seem to be in a perpetual state of hurry these days. We've adopted the mentality that there's so much to do in so little time. We pack our calendars with back-to-back commitments, running from one thing to the next. Hurry, hurry! Everything needs to be fast—the faster the better.

In an era of fast food, we have to be reminded to slow down, eat mindfully, and savor every mouthful. As an antidote to the obesity epidemic we constantly hear about in the news, we're told to sit down at a table for each meal, experience every bite, chew slowly, and put our forks down when we're 80 percent full. It all seems like common sense, but somehow we've gotten away from remembering that food fuels our bodies and that there can be great satisfaction in tasting each morsel. Our choices of what we eat and how we eat our food have to be told to us, such as advice to snack on an apple instead of a bag of chips or to sit down at the dinner table instead of eating on the run in our cars.

A late friend of mine ate her meals at her dining room table. She took time before she ate to prayerfully give thanks for the food before her and for those who had devoted their efforts to growing, picking, packaging, and transporting it so she could enjoy it. When she told me about her meal meditations, I adopted the practice. I also started selecting our food more carefully so it would provide my husband and me with the greatest amount of nourishment possible. With food being delivered to us faster than ever, there's merit in selecting and preparing our meals with care and consuming our food slowly, mindfully, and gratefully.

These days, we also have to be reminded to get moving and break a sweat. We have to be told to get up from our sedentary positions of watching screens large and small and engage in physical activity. There are signs posted on doors to stairwells in a public building I frequent that remind us of the importance of investing in our health. The idea behind the eye-level signs is to encourage people to get some physical activity by taking the stairs instead of the elevator. I am one who favors stairs to elevators. I would rather huff and puff a little to the fourth floor than get complacent and out of shape from taking a ride.

I know the significance of enjoying optimal health, for I have experienced the opposite. I know just how poor I feel when I feel poorly. I have been ill to the point where the idea of walking was too much of a struggle to even contemplate. So now, when I see stairs, they call my name. They serve as my reminder of the true and first wealth of good health. As one who has been paralyzed and had to learn to walk again, I now walk and climb with greater vigor and determination because I have the blessing of being able to do so.

Caring for your health and making changes to enhance your well-being are some of the greatest gifts you can give yourself. When you take care of your body, your healthy habits can't help but radiate inward to the health of your mind and outward to your external beauty. Engaging in self-care is the ultimate expression of self-love. Your health is indeed your most precious possession. Investing in it will yield rich rewards.

What actions do I currently take to care for my health and well-being? Do I focus as much on my inward health as my outward appearance? What lifestyle changes would I like to make that would optimize my health? What small steps can I take today to increase my self-care?

14. WRITE FROM YOUR HEART

I feed my creative spirit by engaging in activities that allow me to express myself.

Our local hospital's auxiliary hosts an annual holiday craft bazaar and bake sale. As I browsed table after table of handmade Christmas tree skirts, fancy knit scarves, and delectable baked goods, I was impressed with the generous sharing of talents. I looked with awe and appreciation at each item, thinking about what it took to make such tempting creations of fabric and yarn and of flour and sugar.

The women on my mother's side of the family have all been skilled with their hands. If you were to have put them all in a room together and encouraged them to work on their latest projects, you would have found my maternal grandmother, mother, aunt, and cousins all displaying their creativity in myriad and beautiful ways.

I think of the other people I know whose creative fires burn, bringing warmth and meaning to the world. One person I know is pursuing photography with gusto, taking classes in order to perfect her craft, while also exploring other aspects of creativity by composing poetry. Another person is quilting in earnest, making elaborate and beautiful works of art and personalized gifts. Yet another person I know is returning to painting, using the brush to create a glorious image of the world.

Creative fires can move people to do great things and surpass previously perceived limits. The dramatic actor stretches himself to try comedy. The classically trained vocalist experiments with a contemporary piece of music. The painter explores a variety of media for self-expression. The photographer changes lenses and captures an image from a different angle. The dancer is weary from practice but emboldened to perform a new dance. The poet finds a new voice through prose.

Without those creative fires and opportunities to stretch ourselves, who would we be? We all have gifts of creativity. We all have talents that invite us to express ourselves in ways that are unique to us and call us to move beyond what we believe about ourselves. I think of a fearless friend whose visits always include her sharing her latest magnificent projects with me. From quilting to looming to painting to constructing, she stretches her boundaries of self-expression every day, and her hands burn with a creative fire.

My own creative fire feeds my soul through music, photography, art, and writing. I enjoy singing solos and duets, and I participate in choirs. I've taken voice and dance lessons, and I've appeared in musicals and plays. I write and I blog. Over the past couple of years, I've taken up nature photography, focusing my lens on close-ups of flowers, leaves, berries, and branches. I also started drawing. By applying colored pencil to paper, exploring shading and color combinations, I've found drawing to be a tremendous creative outlet.

We don't need to become famous or even seek another person's validation of our work. By simply engaging our creative spirits, we realize an important part of our unique selves that needs to be shared with the world.

Here is to the creative spirit in each of us, whether instrumentalist, textile artist, baker, gardener, composer, whatever. Feed your soul. Embrace your uniqueness. Express yourself creatively, joyfully, and bountifully. Do so regularly.

What are my favorite creative pursuits? Do I dedicate enough time to them? How can I make more time to express myself creatively?

15. MAKE YOUR HEART SING

I make room for what gives me joy. By dedicating time
to my passions and pastimes, every day is lighter and
brighter.

I once worked for a business that strongly encouraged its employees
to have clean desk surfaces, in large part because of privacy
issues surrounding the information we dealt with on a regular basis.

While some people are content with a messy desk and can readily
put their hands on a necessary paper among the stacks, I am of the
opposite viewpoint. I think more clearly when I don't have paper and
other clutter surrounding me.

The less there is around me, the better.

I feel free and creative when the physical space around me is open
and light. I also think more clearly in silence. It's as if my space, through
sight or sound, must be clear of distraction in order for my mind to
follow suit.

The same holds true for my calendar. I prefer to have only a few
obligations or tasks needing my concentration and energy each day.
By having space on my calendar, I reserve energy for those things that
make me happy.

When I have time to read, write, sing, draw, take a walk, cook a
healthy meal, attend an interesting lecture or a concert, or spend time
just hanging out with my husband or friends, my heart sings. Therefore,
I free up time on my calendar every day for at least one, if not two or

three or more, of my favorite pastimes in order to balance my day. These activities give me joy. They make my life lighter and brighter.

We all have things that fuel our passions and bring us joy. Sometimes those passions translate into our chosen careers. Whenever possible, find passion in your work. Choose a job that allows you to use your unique gifts. After all, we spend most of our waking hours for much of our lives at work.

At other times, our passions may be in the form of hobbies or items we collect. One summer, I had the pleasure of walking the downtown streets of my community during a classic car show. The historic courthouse square was filled with over a hundred colorful, shining, meticulously detailed classic vehicles ranging from trucks to roadsters, sedans to sports cars. It was obvious some pretty passionate people owned and cared for those vehicles.

Your passion may be teaching or engineering, web design or nursing, classic cars or quilting, gardening or baking, singing or running marathons. Your passions feed your soul and express to the world a glimpse of who you are uniquely. It's not surprising that your passions may be things you're good at or things for which you're often complimented. We have an intuitive sense of what we're good at and what brings zing to our lives.

I know people whose passions have been clearly defined since they were children. Others I know have cultivated them over time, sometimes well into their adulthood. I have a close friend whose passion is art in its many forms. For years, she quilted, sewed, and gardened. These days, her passions have turned to drawing, knitting, and painting. She paints intricate designs on eggs, rocks, and canvases—each a masterpiece.

Whatever your passions are, life becomes richer, fuller, and more meaningful when you fuel them. By realizing your passions and making time for them, you give an exciting gift to yourself and to others.

What makes my heart sing? What gives me joy? What excites me? What are my passions? In what activities do I get so focused that I lose track of time? What am I really good at? What do others think I'm really good at? How might I spend more time on those things I enjoy doing?

16. LIGHTHEARTED

I laugh easily and make time for play every day. The child in me thanks me for it.

If given the opportunity, what advice about life would you give your younger self or someone else you love and care about? Could you reduce that wisdom down to just a few words? Would those words have anything to do with fun, laughter, play, silliness, and joy?

For some people, laughter and play seem to come naturally. They carry that fun spirit with them all of their lives. Others, like me, have to work a bit at having fun.

Fortunately, I'm married to a man who has a grand sense of humor. When he laughs, he has a way of making me laugh too, simply because it's so much fun to see him quiver with joy.

My husband, Larry, frequently awakens laughing in response to his dreams. Rather than suffering through nightmares, his sleep time must be filled with happy, even silly thoughts.

Larry makes our lives together a joyful experience, in part because of his quirky sense of humor. On our first date, for instance, he told me about himself, each story getting more and more interesting, elaborate, and improbable. Finally, he blushed and burst out laughing. Then he informed me that everything he'd just told me had been silliness. It was his way of breaking the ice during the awkwardness of a first date between two thirty-somethings.

Larry and my late father would have gotten along famously. Both men were gifted with a keen intelligence, deep sensitivity, and a generous dose of quirky and clever humor. Dad loved to laugh, and he exuded joy easily, especially around those with whom he was closest. He often could be heard humming throughout the house, and he danced a little jig whenever we had record albums playing on our hi-fi stereo. When I was a child, he drew funny cartoons for me and mailed them to me as surprises when he traveled for his work.

As we grow older, it's natural to see the seriousness of life and to focus our energies there because the weights of worry, heartache, anxiety, and fear find themselves resting squarely on our shoulders. To lessen the gravity, we need to intentionally seek joy and look for opportunities for good, old-fashioned belly laughs, just as my husband does and my father did.

I recommend that you let go of your heavy burdens, if just for a little bit, and expand your bubble.

What's that, you say? Let me explain.

While on my daily walk one midsummer day, I witnessed a little girl singing at the top of her lungs while she watered flowers in front of her home. I laughed along with children who found jumping and splashing in puddles exhilarating entertainment. I watched a little boy run like the wind, not because he had a purpose or particular destination but because he was simply having fun. I delighted in a little girl dancing in bubbles as she blew them. As the bubbles grew, her leaps expanded into them.

I decided then and there that I wanted to expand my own bubble and dance and run and sing and splash just like the children I saw. I wanted time for laughter, play, and relaxation. I wanted to be silly and imaginative. I wanted to be uninhibited. I wanted to be filled with boundless joy.

I realize I'm not alone in that pursuit.

Earlier this year, I facilitated two groups of adults who wanted to move their lives forward with intention. Interestingly, when asked to identify what area of their lives they felt needed the most attention, the subject of play came up again and again. Many of the participants in the two groups wanted more time to play and have fun. They voiced working hard, working long hours, and working with such intensity that little time or energy was left for joyful pursuits.

Despite working hard as a nurse and educator, serving on boards, and doing extensive volunteer work, my late mother was one who laughed easily and enjoyed life. Even in the midst of her many obligations, she made time for play. I heard myself say numerous times after she passed away that the two of us had such fun together.

How often can we say that about our dearest relationships—that we had fun together? I realized that my words said so much about my mom and her philosophy about life. She did have fun, and she made our times together a joyful experience, times that created lifelong memories, times that continue to bring a smile even today when I reflect upon them.

The seriousness of our world can surely weigh us down, where every day brings news of more divisiveness, rancor, tragedy, and violence. Our own smaller worlds may be heavy as well, with sadness, loss, defeat, and trials. We would benefit from lightening up each day, if just for a little while. By doing so, we will bring light into the corners of our world.

We each need to find and make our own joy, sing with abandon, and dance with the expanding bubbles. I urge you to carry summertime in your heart every day, regardless of the season. Focus for just a bit each day on expanding your bubble and making room for laughter, spontaneity, play, and sheer joy. Live, so that one day someone will say how much fun they had when they were with you.

What made me laugh today? How might I make
time each day for relaxation and play?

17. PEACEFUL HEART

I'm at peace with who I am and where I am in my life.
I'm in the right place for right now.

How often do you get caught up in your own world, consumed by even the smallest of irritations? The boss was cranky. The kids are misbehaving. The groceries need to be bought. The laundry needs to be folded. The house is a mess. The dog needs to be walked.

Answer: Breathe. Breathe deeply. Repeat. Repeat again. Breathe in peace. Breathe out peace.

I love the prayer attributed to St. Francis of Assisi that begins with the words, "Lord, make me an instrument of your peace." When my mother passed away, that prayer was included in her memorial service at my request. Afterward, the pastor gave me a laminated version of the prayer, decorated with a colorful image of a stained-glass window. As the pastor handed it to me, she said that my mother's life lived out that prayer. She was an instrument of peace.

For the past few years, I've been dedicating moments before I go to sleep, praying for a greater use of my words and actions and making an intention to be, like my late mom, an instrument of peace.

It isn't always an easy task to release your everyday concerns or make peace with others or yourself, especially if you've done something you aren't proud of. However, peace is a natural state that can be attained despite what is happening inside you or around you.

Simply start by focusing on your breath, breathing in and out, deeply and steadily. Although being seated comfortably with eyes closed is ideal for centering yourself, you can engage in the practice wherever you are, at any time and in any position.

Slow down your breath and release your racing thoughts. Let them fly away, light as feathers. When your mind tries to pick up the threads of those thoughts again, gently release them. There is no judgment, no worry, and no tension.

As you breathe in and out slowly, you will naturally begin to release your stresses. Your body will become more relaxed. You will easily replace any negative thoughts and feelings with more positive, loving, and peaceful versions.

Being at peace is both stabilizing and freeing. It sets the stage for accepting who you are and where you are in your life and knowing with your whole heart that you're in the right place for that very moment. Being in a state of peace doesn't mean you're settling for what you don't want or you're ignoring your desires, goals, or intentions for your life. Instead, such a state gives you the space and permission to start where you are right in the moment and build a new way for yourself.

The turbulence of change, the deep valley of worry, and the loud din of drama will always be there, but we don't have to let them rent space in our minds and hearts. Instead, we can use our energies to become naturally centered in a state of calmness and peace. Only then, when we're free of agitation, distraction, and disturbance, can we truly open ourselves to being instruments of peace.

Spend some time today examining your thoughts, words, and actions and ask yourself if they come from a place of peace.

Where do I need peace? Have I made peace with everything from my past that might have made me unhappy? What action can I take today to feel more peaceful about who and where I am right now?

18. PURE HEART

I fill my spiritual well each day by giving myself
sufficient time for silence, meditation, or prayer.

E very personality indicator test I've ever taken has labeled me an
extrovert. I draw energy from being around other people, especially
when engaged in conversation. Yet there are times when I prefer solitude
and silence. I need that time alone to refill my energy well. When my days
and evenings are filled with busyness, meetings, and other obligations, I
have to stop a bit and become silent and still.

As much as we reach out in our lives, we must reach within. Without
that balance, we have no quiet time for recharging our batteries. When
life is not filled with self- or other-induced busyness, it opens up space
in our lives for healing in all of its manifestations.

Oftentimes, when I'm trying to be silent, the chatter in my head
takes over. It judges, criticizes, and replays events and conversations. It
questions my decisions. It sets the stage for fruitless anxiety, worry, and
regret. At other times, the chatter takes on more of a dreamlike state
where my imagination takes over, creating scenes and fantasies and
filling my head with sugarplums.

To quiet the chatter, whether of the fearful or fanciful variety, I
focus moments each day on my breath. There's nothing formal about it.
I just start focusing on my breath, slowing it down, inhaling and exhaling
deeply. Repeated mindful deep breathing slows all of me down, quieting
my incessant talking mind and moving me toward a more peaceful state.

In addition to mindful breathing, prayer plays an important role in my life. I belong to my church's prayer chain. We receive requests for prayer nearly daily, sometimes multiple times in a day. Rather than confine those prayers to only certain times of the day or evening, I find myself saying little prayers during all of my waking hours. While prayer hopefully spreads good intentions to where they're needed, the practice of praying also quiets and centers me.

The act of walking, especially in nature, has an ability to quiet me as well. I dedicate at least an hour each day during temperate seasons to walking outdoors. Walking is my moving meditation. When I'm walking, I increasingly enter a more mindful state. At first, the chatter in my head will be loud and constant. But as I keep walking, almost as if by magic, the chatter subsides. I hear the birds singing and the wind moving through the trees. The obstacles and impossibilities that were bouncing frantically around in my head just moments ago are suddenly replaced by creative ideas and solutions. I focus on the moment in which I'm living, and the answers come.

Silence and stillness are necessary to our self-nurturing and healing. Being still and silent can reveal and renew. We all need that sacred time. We all need time to be. That is when we touch the infinite and the infinite touches us.

Be still. Be.

Do I allow myself enough time for quiet, rest, and renewal each day? How do I quiet the idle or negative chatter in my head? How might I make more time in my day for silence, meditation, and prayer?

BE STILL YOUR HEART

I accept when I hurt, worry, or am afraid because I know those times are not permanent. I use my experiences with sadness, grief, and loneliness to help others. I'm my own best cheerleader, encouraging myself and others through difficult days. I'm not perfect, and that's okay. I rise above any confusion in my life and find the answers I need. I make decisions with ease and am content with them. My heart is filled with peace.

19. HIDDEN HEART

I release my fears and worries, casting them into the
wind. Once I release my grip on them, they float away.

One Sunday at church, we responsively read text in our worship
bulletins about being blessed. Then we heard the words of
Matthew 5:1–12, words that have come to be known as the Beatitudes.
We heard that those who mourn, those who are meek, those who are
merciful, those who are peacemakers, those who are pure in heart, they
are all blessed.

In our day-to-day living, it's hard at times to remember how
much we, too, are blessed. On that same Sunday morning while in
conversation with two church friends, I was reminded of the meaning
of the Beatitudes text we had all collectively read and heard just minutes
before. One, who was facing the serious illness of an adult child, looked
at me with the calm eyes of faith and said, "Everything will be all right."
The other, a woman who was seeking some changes in her life, gave me
the gifts of her kindness, generosity, and wisdom.

Even in the depths of our sorrow and uncertainty, our fear and
anguish, there is reason to find blessing. At times, we may have to dig a
little deeper, but it's there all the same. Each day that week, I continued
my ritual of beginning and ending my day with three things for which
to be grateful. Such a check-in helps me focus on how much I've been
given in life. I'm blessed with abundance.

I made a comment one day about someone having been given a lot in
life. What I meant at the time was that some people are burdened with

their lot in life, where life seems to be extra hard and good luck difficult to find.

I thought again about my statement and realized I could turn the meaning around to be focused more on blessing than burden. We're each given a lot in life—a lot of good things, that is.

We often get caught up in the hardships, thinking they're permanent when they're not. Our hardships are transient. They eventually go away.

It's also easy to forget each day is blessed with wonderful experiences and gifts. Even some of our hardships can turn out to be gifts as they teach us how to look at our lives with new eyes of appreciation and understanding. We can then choose to live our lives differently because of those newfound lessons and blessings. Having our own lot in life can make us more compassionate and empathetic to the plight of others.

Truly, we're each given a lot in life—a lot of blessings that will almost always overshadow every hidden hurt, fear, or worry. It's what we do with those blessings that matters most.

What hidden hurt, fear, or worry would I like to resolve and heal? How might I reduce its impact on my life? How might I adjust my thinking so I remember that difficult times are impermanent?

20. LONELY HEART

I constructively address my feelings of sadness or grief.
Often, my own hurts diminish when I help someone
else who is suffering.

The human experience, although often ordinary, reveals extraordinary moments of clarity about what matters in life. It's through those extraordinary moments that we come to understand how connected we all are to each other and to each living thing. We learn how that connectedness carries us through some of our most difficult moments.

While at our local farmer's market, my shopping experience was suddenly interrupted by the cries of a little girl. She had stubbed her toe, and her tears came quickly. Her dad, one of the vendors, walked quietly over to the tiny child, asked her what was wrong, embraced her, rubbed her foot, and scooped her up into his arms. His love made all that was wrong better for his small daughter.

I recalled that special time in my life when all that hurt or upset me could instantly be resolved by the love of my parents as they kissed my boo-boos away.

Now that I'm well beyond those years and my parents can no longer kiss me when I'm hurting, I recall those times when others have rallied around me during my pain and sadness. I questioned just how much I reach out or make myself available to others by listening and helping them heal their own hurts and pain.

I may not be able to make it all better for them, but that brief, intimate interaction between a loving father and his little girl gave me some good food for thought about grief, sadness, loneliness, and hurt. That encounter emphasized for me the importance of having empathy and taking action to reach out in kindness to one another. It also made me think of the universality of such experiences when our hearts hurt. We all have them. Those times, which have been aptly described as dark nights of the soul, are part of the growing pains of life.

I have a poised, soft-spoken, and kind friend who shares a mutual love for the works of author Gladys Taber. My friend offered to lend me a particular book of Gladys Taber's from her personal library. *Another Path* confronts the author's sorrow and journey toward healing after the death of her good friend, an experience she called her "storm."

At the time my friend talked with me about our shared literary interests, I was slowly healing from my own grief storm that began when my mother became ill and subsequently passed away. Slowly, the storm was subsiding to more of a dark night. Like the dawn of each new day, light was incrementally making its presence on my horizon once again. I was beginning to see the light of all that is truly everlasting.

We all go through storms, dark nights, and shadows. Life doesn't let us get by without experiencing them, without suffering from our own grief wounds. What we do with our sadness, our loneliness, our hurt, and our grief is what's important. If we allow ourselves to fully embrace the experience, as painful as it may be, we'll move through it. It may be difficult at times during that awkward dance with grief, for the steps go backward and forward and sideways, and then backward again, and then finally forward. Seeking support during that awkward dance will help make the steps come easier.

We have the choice to accept our sorrows, allow ourselves to grieve, and, with time, let go of what was in exchange for something new. At the same time, we receive reassurance from those things that remain unchanged, such as love, a new day, and the passing of the storm to a place of sunshine once again.

If we choose to grow from our difficulties, we'll open the door to becoming more empathetic, compassionate, considerate, and appreciative. Our suffering can transform us into better versions of ourselves.

What healthy, healing ways can I identify that will help me deal with any loneliness, sadness, or grief I am carrying in my heart? How might I help another person who is suffering?

21. GET TO THE HEART OF IT

I release confusion in my life by taking positive steps toward clarity. My head and heart guide me to the right answers.

Life can be compared to a roller-coaster ride with its share of twists and turns, thrills and chills, peaks and valleys, slow ascents and rapid declines. The peaks are exhilarating, while the valleys, those deep places in which we find ourselves when we're uncertain, confused, sad, or despondent, force us to ponder solutions so we can gain a clear path up and out again.

Those emotional valleys are not fun places to stay for very long, but we need them in order to better appreciate the mountaintops of clarity and joy where we break through the clouds and the sun shines brightly.

I believe the valleys of our lives are important indicators of things that require change. They're also the place of temporary setbacks that stop us and force us to reframe the situation and then lead us into new, more appropriate and promising directions.

It's natural to dislike being in any state of discomfort. However, I wouldn't recommend marching out of the valley too quickly just to avoid the pain. I believe you must fully experience those moments and derive from them the valuable lessons they provide in order for you to live a real and complete life. What you learn from those experiences and how you use that knowledge to live a better life and help others on their life journeys is even more important.

How might you confront those confusing times in productive and positive ways? I believe the answer is held in your head and in your heart—your intellect and your intuition.

You are gifted with problem-solving skills. You have the ability to draw upon your experiences and knowledge to help you find your way. You use those same skills when you consult others for support to help you identify potential solutions. Seeking the assistance of trusted supporters can help you gain clarity and direction.

You are also gifted with intuition. That quiet, wise voice deep inside of you can help you find your way out of confusion. You just have to become silent and listen.

When I have major decisions to make, I draw from both my head and heart, but I must admit that I rely pretty heavily on my heart. Perhaps that's why I've been finding so many heart-shaped stones, puddles, leaves, and other objects on my daily walks over the past year. During that same time, I've pondered some pretty big decisions—some confusing at times, including whether to write this book and, if so, what I should write that would best convey my life's journey and help others with theirs.

My head and heart have a better chance of communicating with me when I take long walks. So walking I did. With each step, I kept listening for what might speak to my heart, confident the answer would come out of the silence. And the answer came. In fact, it came so decisively and clearly that this book practically wrote itself with very little effort or intervention from me. The words and concepts poured out of me onto the page. I knew I was on the right path.

When you find yourself in a valley of indecision, confusion, sorrow, challenge, or uncertainty, draw answers from outside and inside of yourself. Tap into your intellect and your intuition. Then use your ingenuity. As you take action, you'll soon find yourself up on the clear mountaintop with the clouds below you and the sun shining on your face once again.

What feels confusing in my life? What steps might I take to find clarity?

22. DISCERNING HEART

*I listen to where I'm being called. I joyfully turn the
page to the next chapter in my life.*

E very day we're confronted with decisions. Most of them are small
and are made without much thought, such as selecting a parking
space or choosing what to make for dinner.

Some decisions, however, are so big, so serious that they warrant
our full attention and careful thought.

Some decisions are private and happen deep in our hearts. Others
are more public and may involve other people's approval.

There are those decisions that prove difficult to make because of
fear of repercussion or other consequences. At times the easier, though
potentially not best, decision is made with safety and status quo in mind.
After all, who wants to step outside of your comfort zone and welcome
skeptics who might judge your decision-making capabilities?

I've periodically made career decisions that some have called exciting
and invigorating, while others have used such terms as courageous and
fearless.

After more than fifteen years on one job I found fun and exhilarating,
I realized my heart was calling me elsewhere. That awareness drew me
to another job I loved more than I could have ever imagined for another
twelve years. But then my heart called again, and I left that career for
another new adventure.

Both times, I realized I couldn't ignore the nudges I'd been feeling. I
needed to pursue my next dream. Admittedly, I considered my decisions

carefully and prayerfully for months and months, but the appeal of listening to my heart and then heeding it always won out.

The experiences I've had with life-threatening and life-altering illnesses have heightened my awareness of just how fragile and fleeting life can be. Therefore, I want to make sure, when all is said and done, I won't leave this life regretting I didn't pursue the next exciting chapter when it presented itself.

I must admit there are those decisions that seem right at the time but may not prove to be a great fit in the long run. Rather than beating yourself up over what you perceive as a mistake, adjust your way of thinking about the experience. You'll see the decision was right for the time, and it still is. Your decision likely provided an opportunity for you to learn and grow and try something new. It may have even moved you into a new direction you could have never seen for yourself otherwise. After all, there may be several right decisions and you simply selected the one that appeared best at the time.

I once responded to the call of a brain teaser published in a newsletter I receive. After some contemplation, I found a solution to the puzzle but not without first examining the absolutes and tossing away my assumptions. Interestingly, if I looked at the puzzle one way, I could arrive at the correct answer. If I looked at it another way, I could also arrive at the right answer.

My preference was for the latter. (Maybe it's my left-handed view on life.) I simply got to the correct answer by taking a different route, laying out a different scenario of possibilities just by allowing for one clue to be treated as factual, not literal. Purists might say my alternative interpretation was wrong, but I like my unconventional approach. Every clue fit into place using that other route.

The brain twister challenged me to look at how I make decisions and through what lens I view my everyday world. How often do I truly look at the absolutes without biases? How readily do I identify and toss aside my assumptions in order to come to a better conclusion? How often do I look at a challenge creatively, taking an unconventional approach to get to the right answer?

Life can be an adventure of growing and learning. Each day can offer the turning of a new chapter in your book of life. Where might the next page turn for you?

What decision is weighing on my heart? What prevents me from making that decision? What constructive action might I take today to help me make my decision?

23. FORGIVING HEART

I'm not perfect, and that's okay. I'm a work in progress.
I forgive myself easily and completely.

As a child, I was taught the fundamental lesson of forgiveness.
When I forgive, I feel free, uplifted, and filled with love. Sadly, I
find it much easier to forgive another person than to forgive myself. I
believe it comes from an unrealistic, self-induced pressure I've learned
over time as I attempt to achieve an unattainably high standard. It's an
unhealthy drive that's led me to a tendency toward perfectionism all of
my life. No one else has ever applied that pressure on me—no parent,
no teacher, only me. What a senseless burden. Indeed, I'm a type A
personality.

My employers have perhaps liked this tendency in me, for it has
driven me to a higher quality of work with less risk for error or waste.
The pursuit of perfectionism, however, is a slippery slope. In an effort to
not make any mistakes, to never fail, to have everything in its place and
assume maximum control of everything, including the uncontrollable,
you only rob yourself of the joy of experimenting, learning, and enjoying
the elegant clumsiness of the journey. That's where the magic takes
place.

Perfectionism seems to be rooted in the outcome, as if everything
rests on it. Surely, the end result is important, but so is the journey to
that end result. That's what makes life exciting and fun, and where new
ideas and insights grow and flourish.

And what is perfect anyway? My definition of what's perfect is likely different from yours. Do I even recognize perfection when I see it? Probably not. I'm too tied up in knots, trying to make things go the way I think they're supposed to go that I may not even recognize when it's going well because I have too many expectations—of me. Perfectionism can be paralyzing and dispiriting.

When I see myself starting to head down that dreaded perfection path, I get disgusted. I should know better. However, such thinking only builds a wall.

That's when I stop for a moment, take a deep breath, and even laugh. I acknowledge that I'm doing my best. I forgive myself, and then I move on, releasing my unrealistic expectations. That little bit of distancing from the situation really helps. It becomes a bridge rather than a wall.

I once heard an interesting presentation about bridges and walls. Afterward, I pondered the many times in my life when I've attempted to build walls as a protective measure around me. I thought I'd be safe and free from hurt, risk, and my perfectionistic tendencies. If only I could construct a wall that was strong enough and high enough to be impenetrable.

As the years have gone by, my perspective has changed. I now realize building a wall is a rather fruitless effort on my part. I can never totally be free from hurt, risk, or disappointment. In fact, in building a wall, I run the greater risk of shutting out love, fun, adventure, and spontaneity. That's the stuff of life's greatest rewards.

A far better exercise is to build a bridge. Bridges help you reach out to another person, meet new friends, and develop new understandings. Bridges lead you to cultivating new interests, exploring new ideas, and perhaps even teaching you a few things about yourself. Bridges can lead to forgiveness.

I suggest we build bridges to lift others up when they're in pain. Build bridges to those who may have wronged us. Build bridges to those parts of ourselves that hurt. Tear down any walls you perceive around you. Become a bridge of loving forgiveness. It may very well be your most rewarding construction.

What do I need to forgive about myself? How would I feel if I released my grudges, anger, disappointments, and resentment for just today? Am I a perfectionist? What does perfection mean to me? How would I feel about myself and my life if I were able to forgive and let go of my perfectionistic tendencies?

24. TAKE HEART

I affirm my values, thoughts, decisions, and actions.
I'm my own best cheerleader. I offer encouragement
to myself and others.

I'm named after my maternal grandmother. She was considered "Big Carrie," and I was "Little Keri" until I grew to be the taller of the two of us.

If I close my eyes, I can see Grandma Carrie. I think of Christmas and the stacks of large coffee cans she filled with a wide array of fancy cookies. I see her beautifully decorated home in shades of olive that felt both elegant and cozy. I see the pressed flower note cards she made. I think of birthday cakes and holiday dinners. I see small, slender trays on which I ate my breakfast in her living room while watching Saturday morning cartoons. I think of fingernail polish and fashionable pantsuits. I see the writing desk she kept in her bedroom where she would pen heartfelt notes to those she loved and cared about.

Most of all, I think of Grandma Carrie's words for me when I was a young girl, encouraging me to embrace my gifts and talents and become the person I was meant to be. She wrote those words in a greeting card in celebration of a special time in my life. She included a favorite poem about hope and faith and a handwritten note filled with love and encouragement. It's among my most precious keepsakes.

We all benefit from encouragement along life's journey, and we all have the ability to encourage someone else at any time. Although

Grandma Carrie probably didn't realize how much her encouraging words meant to me, they've stayed with me through the decades.

When I feel my hope or confidence fading, I remember Grandma's note and her favorite poem. I recall the loving words and gestures of others who have kindly supported me throughout the years and who continue to support me today. They are the "forever" people in my life who are there through thick and thin. They are the acquaintances who are there at just the right time with just the right words. I strive to be that same type of support to others, but it can seem hard. There are times when I don't know what to do for those who are hurting. I feel inadequate.

A dear friend went through a difficult period marked by numerous life-changing events: the marriage of a child, the death of a parent, and then her own illness. During the depths of her sorrow, a mutual friend and I stood with her in silence, each holding one of her hands. I recall feeling utterly helpless, not knowing what I could do to ease my friend's pain. Yet she told me months later that she derived strength and encouragement from that simple act of our holding her hands, standing in silence together. Because of it, she said, she was better able to face her challenges.

Our words of encouragement and gestures of caring can speak much louder than we ever realize. When we know the benefits of such warmth in our own lives, I believe we should pay it forward to someone else whenever and in whatever way we can.

Don't forget to spread that kindness and encouragement to yourself as well. Develop the habit of being your own cheerleader, especially during difficult times. Saying a kind word and affirmation of support to your reflection in a mirror can do wonders.

Who's to say that your gesture of encouragement, large or small, might not be just what you or another person needs today?

Where in my life do I need encouragement? Who needs encouragement from me?

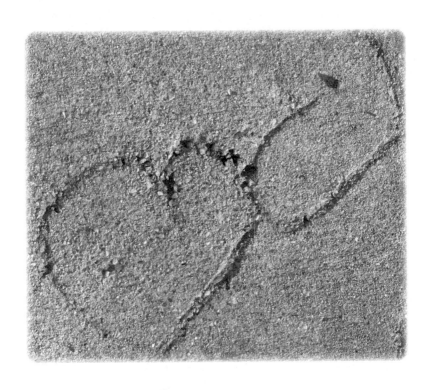

FOLLOW YOUR HEART

I accept what is, and I trust my place in this journey of life. I'm open to change, confident that good things await me. I let go of what's no longer needed in my life, freeing myself to receive all that's new. I tap into my intuition for wisdom. In a state of quietness and patience, I listen for the message of my calling. I'm no longer afraid to stretch outside of my comfort zone. I take positive action with ease. I gladly and willingly follow my heart.

25. CHANGE OF HEART

I embrace change, which opens exciting, new doors
for me.

There are times when a word or concept comes into my life
repeatedly for a short period. I'm challenged to pay attention to it
and determine what it means to me.

So it was with the word "impermanence." Over and over, I
encountered that word for a period of weeks, often accompanied by
the wisdom that we must accept and embrace impermanence in order
to find peace and open ourselves to newness. A certain amount of trust
is required.

There are admittedly times when I think things will last forever,
never changing. The truth is that things are changing constantly, even
if in small increments. Look at nature, which is in a constant state
of change. The seasons of the year give us a great example, from the
awakening and renewal of spring to the greening and growing of summer
to the harvesting and dying away of autumn to the quiet and dormancy
of winter.

I used to spend needless time trying to resist change when I thought
it came too fast or with too hard of a knock or I wasn't the one initiating
it. If I had my way, life's changes would happen more slowly and subtly,
and I would have more control over them.

But you're not always given that option. Some things are outside
of your control. What you can control, however, are your thoughts.
When you recognize your worries for what they are, they become more

manageable. They are only thoughts after all. What matters is how you choose to respond to them.

Once I came to accept there is no stopping change and I may or may not be in control of that change, I learned to let go. Truly, everything and everyone is in a state of impermanence, including the people and the things you love. You are impermanent too.

When you choose to let go and embrace impermanence, instead of digging in your heels and resisting, you gain an increased sense of internal stability and a clearer view. Letting go is liberating. It doesn't mean you have to settle for what you don't want in life. It means you have the power to rise above what feels difficult or challenging. Letting go enables you to recalibrate your perspective so you can move more effectively, creatively, and mindfully through your present moments.

Now. Now is truly all you have. To reflect too heavily upon the past or project too far into the future only robs you of the present moment. By contrast, when you are in that state of now and a state of flow that allows you to move elegantly with and through change, you accept where you are in the moment and life feels easier. Consequently, your burdens lessen because the tension is released. Fear, regret, and worry lose their hold over you. Change loses its threat. The energy of creativity and possibility replaces it.

Surely, it can feel scary to face change and something new. Staying where you no longer fit or where you no longer want to be, however, is worse. Rather than focusing on the old, find the possibilities in the present moment. An intentional change in perspective right now can lead to the development of a better future. Letting go helps you hear that small, still voice deep inside of you that may be calling you to new things or new insights. As if in response, the act of embracing change allows for new doors to open, doors you might have never imagined possible.

When you reframe your perspective and jump in with both feet— or at least take one small step or even a tiptoe—into change, you set the stage for newness. Such openness to new things may involve risk, reinvention, a setback or obstacle, or energy you may not be certain you have. But it can also be that special something you need in order to reinvigorate or redirect your life onto a new and more interesting and fulfilling path.

Everything is impermanent—everything. When you know that and you embrace change and you allow the flow of life to take you along with it, amazing things happen. Have faith and enjoy the journey.

What is my attitude about change? What do I need to change in my life? What action might I take to make that change? If I were to alter my thoughts about change, what might happen?

26. OPEN HEART

> I release negative energy by accepting what is instead of
> staying stuck in how I think things should be. I open
> my heart to new insights. As a result, my life expands.

When you live in a cold-weather climate, there's nothing as lovely as opening windows for the first time in the spring and letting in fresh air. My routine spring tasks include sweeping out the mounds of sand from the garage floor that accumulated over months of snow, washing winter salt off of the car, and putting screens back on casement windows. I practically dance whenever I do these chores, for it means one thing: spring! Warmer weather is on the way. It's a time of newness.

It's been our habit in recent years to remove the screens from our home's windows in the fall, scrubbing them clean and then storing them for the winter so we can get the most out of the precious daylight streaming through our windows during the long, dark months. Whenever I hear the temperature is supposed to soar back into the sixties, I wash the insides of the windows, reinstall the screens, and then let the fresh breezes in to release the stale, cooped-up winter air.

Such activity makes me think of the stale energy that might be cooped up and cluttering my mind and heart.

A few years ago, I didn't want to admit I was stuck in a rut. Things were difficult in my life at that time between my own illness and caring for a dying parent. I felt stuck in chaos. In looking back, however, I realize I was indeed stuck in a rut. I was stuck in the mind-set of how I thought things ought be in my life, not how they actually were.

Once I identified my true feelings and set into motion some new thoughts, I opened my mind and heart, letting go of the difficult things that weighed me down. That new perspective brought about an acceptance and gratitude that helped me through a tough time. Rather than staying stuck in how I thought things should be, I found peace in what was.

When I breathe in gratitude and change my way of thinking, it's as if that old energy dissipates and a new, affirming energy sweeps in to take its place. I grow by gaining new insights. Where I was stuck, there is now release. The windows of my world become clearer and brighter. The so-called salt and sand stuck in the crevices of my old mind-set are swept away. That's one type of cleaning that doesn't have to wait until spring.

Where in my life do I need to open my mind and heart? What do I need to accept in my life as it is? Where might I be stuck in an old way of thinking that is no longer productive for me? Where do I need to reframe my thinking or gain a new perspective or insight?

27. CLEAN HEART

I let go of what I no longer need. A clean space and mind allow for something new to enter my life.

I've read time and again that we clear our thoughts and pave the way for newness in our lives when we rid ourselves of things we no longer need. Some experts on the subject suggest boxing things up you're no longer using but can't part with. Mark a date for a year from now on the box and then store it. If you haven't dug into it by the due date, simply take the box, still sealed, to the nearest thrift store and donate it.

Other experts say you should clear out anything that doesn't make you happy or doesn't add beauty to your life. Yet others suggest you should go through a cleaning spree, ridding yourself of a certain number of items every day for a certain number of days.

I love the idea of cleaning and organizing, ridding myself of things no longer needed but in good condition. It allows for those unneeded items to be enjoyed by someone else. I tend to live a lean life without a lot of stuff around me. I'm simply happier living simply.

But what about the intangible stuff we carry around with us?

It was a slate-gray, windy, and rainy Sunday, and I was home in my pajamas and robe, snuggled in my chair, coughing, blowing my nose, and suffering from aches and chills. The weather and my body seemed to be accurate reflections of each other. A spring cold was not on my to-do list.

While I missed several scheduled events due to this unwelcome cold visiting me, I decided to use my quiet time to do some spring cleaning. Unlike the physical exertions of washing curtains, removing clutter from closets, and scrubbing down cupboards and walls, this spring cleaning involved ridding myself of the clutter in my mind.

First of all, I searched for those things lurking around in the recesses that didn't contribute to my well-being. I found I had a more-than-generous load of assumptions, expectations, and old sorrows that were only weighing me down.

As I searched some more, I uncovered grudges, judgments, and over-commitments. There were stresses, uncertainties, fears, worries, negative thoughts, sad memories, and statements I wished I could take back.

With eyes closed, I visualized unloading those burdens that were causing me so much harm and creating in me a sense of dis-ease. I evaluated each concern and worked to frame it more positively, turning fear into hope, sorrow into gratitude, and stress into peace. My evaluation also converted uncertainty into clarity, worry into joy, crisis into opportunity, and old hurts into new understandings. I was amazed at how hard it was to let go of those burdens. (Why did I still want to own them?) As I released them little by little, my mind, body, and spirit felt healthier.

Who would have guessed that a cold, in all of its untimeliness and unpleasantness, could actually end up being the gift of such necessary spring cleaning?

Consider spending time today removing the tangible and intangible clutter from your life.

What new habit would I like to start? What current habit would I like to break? What do I need to let go of? What is cluttering my life? How might I get started today to clear and clean and start anew?

28. CURIOUS HEART

I'm comfortable stepping outside of my comfort zone.
That's where life's adventures begin.

The fortune cookie message read: "A good time to start something new." It was a warm, sunny afternoon, and my husband and I had decided to hike at one of our favorite places. Butterflies danced around us, birds sang, and the changing autumn leaves whispered as the trees swayed gently over our heads.

Few hikers take to the paths in that particular spot, and those who do never leave debris or garbage behind. So when I saw a piece of paper along the path, I quickly picked it up, prepared to put it in my pocket and toss it in the trash after we got home. As I picked up the small piece of paper, however, I recognized it as a fortune from a cookie. "A good time to start something new," it read. A message meant for me!

I'd been stretching my comfort zone at that time in my life, and I'd discovered that trying something new was exhilarating. The treasure found in someone's fortune cookie on the path that day was just the reinforcement I needed that my own personal paths were taking me right where I was supposed to be.

It's been said the more scared you are of your calling, the greater the reason to pursue it. There can be something uncomfortable, scary, and risky about stepping outside of your comfort zone into something new. But if it's calling you, it will continue to call you, first quietly, then a little louder, and then so loudly that you may not be able to ignore it anymore. The fear that comes from the prospect of trying something new is eclipsed by a deep knowledge that you not only want to pursue that something new, you somehow have to do it, as if you're drawn to it like a magnet. Knowing you have to pursue it and then doing so can produce some of life's most rewarding moments.

Moving outside of your comfort zone doesn't have to mean something unconventional or radical, such as quitting your job, divorcing your spouse, selling all of your belongings, and moving halfway across the country or world. It can simply mean taking a class to learn a new skill or subject, volunteering your time for a cause or organization that's new to you, or devoting time to a hobby you've wanted to try. Then again, moving outside of your comfort zone might be one of those watershed moments when life is calling you in a different direction entirely.

I read an article about a man who experienced such a turning point in his life. He decided he had reached a stage where it was important to give back. Consequently, he reinvented himself to do just that, leaving his comfort zone totally behind. He took a risk that would give him renewed vigor, satisfaction, and rewards of the everlasting, not tangible, kind. He responded to his calling despite his comfort zone urging him to stay put.

We all have our comfort zones. We get stuck in our ruts, afraid of change and what that change might do to transform us. We crave the reassurance and so-called stability of the tried and true. Over time, however, those ruts can cause us to feel unhappy and unfulfilled, even complacent with our lives. We might begin to question if that's all there is.

I say that's the ideal moment for a new adventure. The discomfort that comes from feeling unfulfilled may be just what is needed to force the door open to assessing your life, searching for your truth, and finding your way.

Take the risk. Heed the call. Step outside of your comfort zone to a new place of adventure, be it big or small. What are you waiting for? It's a good time to start something new.

What new adventure or activity is calling to me?
What subject would I like to learn more about? What
new skill would I like to learn? What would my life
look like if I stepped outside of my comfort zone and
tried something new?

29. HEART MAGNET

*I focus my intentions with specificity to attract what
I desire in my life.*

The older I get, the more I embrace the mysteries of life, including
a deepening connection to loved ones from my past. One day
when particularly perplexed about something, I desperately wanted a
conversation with my late mother. Her advice always made things right
again.

So I tossed my intention into the universe, and it was answered.
My "conversation" with Mom came through a book by Gladys Taber,
her favorite author. After sending out my intention, I was drawn to
look at the Gladys Taber books I inherited when my mother passed
away. There, in lightly penciled notations in the book's margins and
in the brackets drawn around specific passages, I was able to find the
quiet counsel I'd been seeking. There was the gentle, loving advice that
sounded as if it were coming from Mom's lips to my ear.

Our intentions are powerful. We're magnets that can attract
amazing things into our lives when we're specific, clear, present, and
trusting. The force of the universe makes it possible for us to attract
that which we seek.

I frequently articulate such intentions, framing them less as wants
or needs and more as things already manifested. And then I wait. Some
of my intentions are answered immediately, and others take more divine
time until they appear—often even better than I could have imagined.

One such time when my intention was immediately manifested was when my mother was dying. She was in the final stage of cancer, and we were within hours of her passing. By that point, she was in a deep sleeping state, and the time for conversation was past. Still, I talked to her, reminisced to her, stroked her arm, touched her face, read aloud from her favorite books, and sang to her the songs she used to sing to me when I was a small child. The nursing home's staff turned on the television in her room to a cable channel featuring easy-listening music in order to create a soothing environment for us both.

I listened to the music and felt sad and alone and rather afraid. I had sent my husband home. He had been so devoted, but it was time now for me to sit quietly with Mom and be there with her when she passed away.

I'm an only child, and I'd been unusually close to both of my parents. In my alone time with Mom that evening, I prayed my late father would be with us during that time of goodbye. I asked for a sign from him so I would know. I needed to have the comfort that as I let go of Mom's hand, he would be there to take it. So I tossed my intention out into the universe.

I had just about given up that I would receive a sign from Dad, thinking I was rather silly, when suddenly my ear tuned to the easy-listening music on the television. What I heard was the signature piece of music from a television show on which my father had appeared for many years. I had never heard that piece of music played anywhere except in association with that television show until that night with my mom.

My request had been answered. I had received my sign. Dad was there, and I knew it. I could feel his presence. The three of us were in different states of being—Mom, Dad, and me—but we were indeed there as a family. Almost instantly, I was pulled from the depths of my fear and grief into a state of peaceful acceptance. My intention had been answered even better than I could have imagined. The mysterious transition from life to death was under way for Mom, and Dad was there to comfort and guide us both through it.

If you were a magnet, what would you like to attract into your life? What intention would you like to have fulfilled? (Be as clear and specific as possible. Word it in the present tense, as if it has already been manifested.) What beliefs do you have that could limit your manifesting that which you wish to attract? What action might you take to manifest what you desire and believe?

30. FOLLOW YOUR HEART

I listen to that wise voice deep inside me. It never lets me down.

It was the first day of Epiphany at church, a day celebrated in the Christian tradition when the three kings were to have visited the infant Christ child. We started the worship service with the congregation singing "We Three Kings," repeating after each verse the refrain that concludes with "guide us to Thy perfect light."

In addition to its religious significance, epiphany holds a more secular meaning, such as when a bell seems to go off and you suddenly have clarity about something. Without warning, you're guided to the light of understanding. You grasp something intuitively that had up until that point remained unknown.

I was asked to speak to a group of nursing professionals about the role of intuition in our spiritual maturity journey. The topic came naturally to me because I'm a strong believer in my intuition and the importance it plays in my decision-making process. I often have epiphanies.

I'm guided by the light of my intuition in all areas of my life. I listen to that inner voice for all things and find it has been spot-on over and over again. I've learned through trial and error that it's well worth it for me to listen and heed its wise messages, even when those messages seem strange and unfounded. I just have to trust that my intuition is guiding me, and at some point, I'll understand where it's taken me and why.

That deep wisdom has carried me through some difficult experiences with my health. I'm grateful for what I call "the doctor within" that has nudged me to pay attention to subtle signals in my body. On two separate occasions, I was told that I saved my life by listening to those signals and conveying them with confidence and conviction to medical professionals. Both times, I brought vague but persistent health concerns to physician specialists that revealed unexpected, life-saving outcomes.

The first occasion came when I insisted to a medical oncologist that I needed a second mastectomy. A prophylactic procedure was approved. While the surgery seemed straightforward at the time, it ended up revealing a small malignant tumor hidden from the scrutinizing diagnostic view of a mammogram.

The second occurrence took place when I expressed concern to my dermatologist about a small, shiny, pink spot on my right ankle. Much to his surprise, the dermatologist informed me after removing that innocuous-looking pink spot that it was actually a type of melanoma lacking pigmentation.

When asked by my doctors later what drew me to those subtle signals that on the surface appeared to have no medical merit, I responded that I had no idea except I felt compelled to do so. Both times, the physicians informed me that by listening to my body and following my heart, I saved my life—twice. My intuition is truly my trusted "doctor within."

I also consult that same inner wisdom regularly when making other major and minor decisions. It's there where I tune into my heart or follow my gut, if you will. I still use my intellect when making decisions, but my head and heart have to be in alignment for the decision to feel right.

I told the nursing professionals during my speaking engagement that day that I believe the loud, linear mind can tell you only a portion of truth. I believe there is another deeper, inexplicable truth that comes to you when you don't allow the voice of inner wisdom to be out-shouted by your intellect or ego. It is then when your confused and uncertain self can find answers. When you become still and silent, you make way for the soul to speak and lead you to the right path. What had previously been elusive suddenly is illuminated with the light of clarity. Epiphany.

Once you receive that illumination, what next? That's the invitation to tune into and follow your heart. You begin by listening to that small, still voice deep within. As epiphany comes, you see a light for your path. You know what action to take. You trust it and you follow it, moving more and more into your truth. Out of what may seem like nowhere, your passions and purpose easily reveal themselves. Solutions to difficult problems come readily. Answers to questions you haven't even asked yet find you. Otherwise senseless fragments align, forming a new understanding. You become someone new. You become someone who lives from your heart. Epiphany.

Spend more time in silence. Ask to be guided by the light of your intuition. Tune into your heart. The voice of deep wisdom called truth will speak to you. Then release your fears, do what your intuition guides you to do, and follow your heart.

How do I feel when I listen to my intuition? What happens when I follow its guidance? What have been the ramifications when I haven't followed my intuition? What is my heart saying to me today? How might I live a life that is true to my heart (where my passions and purpose reside)? What steps might I take to follow my heart?

MOVING FORWARD
WITH YOUR WHOLE HEART

Now that you've read the heart-inspired essays, considered the affirmations, and responded to the questions, what might you do next? Here's what I would suggest:

Reread the affirmations and adopt those that resonate with you as your own. Repeat them daily upon awakening, every time you look in a mirror, and right before you go to bed.

Read the essays once again and identify thoughts and phrases that speak to you.

Read through your responses to the questions again, again, and maybe again. Look for common themes and overlaps. Look for aha moments—those things that surprise you. Write down your observations.

Select one or two ideas from your writings that speak loudly to you, ideas you'd like to pursue in order to create your abundant, authentic, joyful life.

Write down those ideas and then write one step you can take now to get you started on each of them. Add a desired outcome and why it's desired. Add a deadline. Hold yourself accountable.

Then sit quietly and set your intentions with your whole heart for your special, chosen ideas. Visualize them. See them as real. See them as happening now.

Finally, take action on the first step you've laid out for each of your ideas. That first step is often the hardest, but once taken, it makes the rest of the path brighter and easier to navigate.

When you feel comfortable with your pursuit of your one or two chosen ideas, go back again to your responses to the questions and repeat the process, selecting one or two more ideas for action and then a couple more ideas, and then a couple more, until you've worked your way through all of your responses.

As you journey forward, making one idea after another come alive, your life will continue to shape and reshape into one of your own creation—one of abundance, authenticity, and joy.

Start today. See the possibilities. Believe in yourself.

Find your heart. Follow your heart.

Printed in the United States
By Bookmasters